little & LARGE
sticker activity book

HORSES & PONIES

BARDFIELD
PRESS

First published by Bardfield Press in 2005
Copyright © Miles Kelly Publishing Ltd 2005

Bardfield Press is an imprint of
Miles Kelly Publishing Ltd
Bardfield Centre, Great Bardfield, Essex, CM7 4SL

2 4 6 8 10 9 7 5 3 1

Editorial Director: Belinda Gallagher

Project Manager: Lisa Clayden

Designer: Tom Slemmings

Production Manager: Estela Boulton

British Library Cataloguing-in-Publication Data
A catalogue record for this book is available from the British Library

ISBN 1-84236-514-2

Printed in China

ACKNOWLEDGEMENTS

The publishers would like to thank the following artists
who have contributed to this book:

Steve Caldwell, Andrea Morandi, Rudi Vizi

Other images: Acquie Image Media, Lisa Clayden, Corel Corporation,
Horseware Ireland, Shires Equestrian Products

www.mileskelly.net
info@mileskelly.net

Introduction

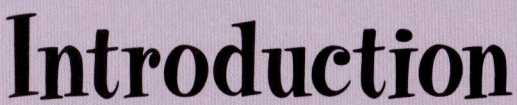

Horses and ponies have always been important to humans. When they were first tamed, horses had two main jobs: strong horses would pull heavy loads and fast horses were used for travel.

Even though we now have tractors and cars to do these jobs, horses and ponies are still very popular, from the giant Shire horse to the miniature Shetland pony.

With this great sticker book you can learn all about horses and ponies and amaze your friends with equine facts!

Mini stickers!

Which breed of horse is the tallest? Why do horses wear metal shoes on their feet? What type of hat do Western riders traditionally wear?

Use your mini stickers to find out about horses and ponies, how to care for them, their relatives and the work they do.

In the field – many horses are kept outside in a field

Relatives – these animals are closely related to horses and ponies

Horse care – equipment that is very important when looking after a horse

At work – different jobs that horses and ponies can do

In the field

▲ Shetland pony

▲ Skewbald pony

▲ Pony friends

▲ Grey pony

▲ Exmoor pony

▲ Appaloosa mare and foal

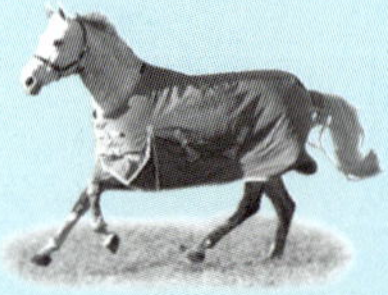

▲ Cantering horse

▲ Horse in winter

▲ Haflinger mare and foal

▲ Arab horse

▲ Bay horses

▲ Chestnut pony

Relatives

▶ Donkey foal

▶ Zebra and foal

Horse care

▲ Apples

▲ Saddle

▲ Riding hat

▲ Horseshoe

▲ Grooming Kit

▲ Tack

At work

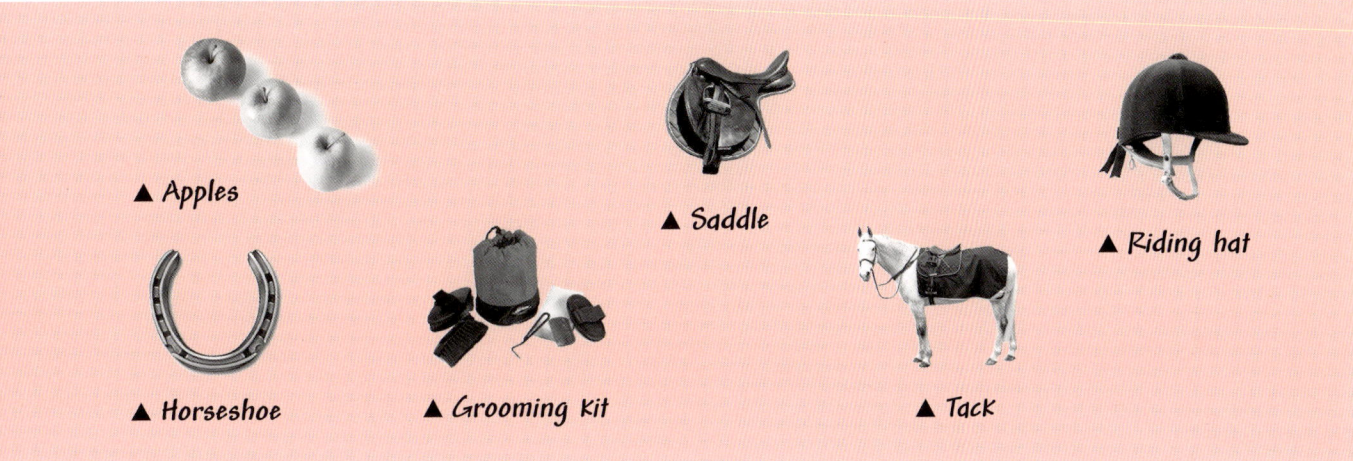

▲ Shire horse

▲ Lipizzaner

▲ Eventing

▲ Polo pony

▲ Driving pony

▲ Mounted games

▲ Morgan horse

▲ Racehorse

▲ Western riding

▲ Heavy horses

▲ Hackney

▲ Barrel racing

Horses and ponies

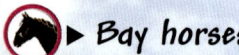 **▶ Bay horses**
These horse are bay coloured – this means they have a brown body and a dark mane and tail

▼ Driving pony
Driving is a popular horse sport – the pony needs to be fit and strong to pull the vehicle

▶ Polo pony
The game of polo requires a fast pony that is obedient and agile

▶ Zebra and foal
Zebras are closely related to the modern horse

◀ Horseshoe
Metal horseshoes help protect a horse's feet

◀ Shetland pony
A small pony, the Shetland is thought to be the strongest for its size

 ▶ Grooming Kit
A grooming kit should include brushes to help keep your pony clean

▲ Exmoor pony
Exmoor ponies are thought to have existed since prehistoric times, but today they are a rare breed

KEY:

 In the field

 Horse care

 At work

 Relatives

◄ Chestnut pony
The colour chestnut varies from a reddish brown through to a deep reddish gold

◄ Pony friends
Ponies enjoy the company of other horses and ponies

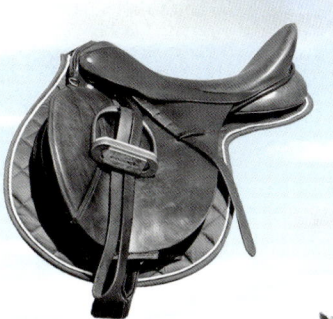

► Donkey foal
A male donkey is called a Jack and a female is called a Jenny

► Saddle
A well-fitting saddle is essential for the comfort of the horse

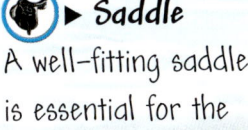

► Lipizzaner
These powerful horses are used in the Spanish Riding School

◄ Horse in winter
In cold weather, horses may need to wear a protective rug to keep them warm

► Skewbald
This pony's coat is made up of patches of brown and white – this colour combination is called skewbald

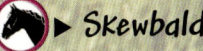

◄ Western riding
This Western rider is wearing a traditional Stetson hat

The Romans used a type of iron sandal on their horses' feet!

Drive off!

 Horses and ponies can be taught to pull a special vehicle – often called a driving carriage or gig.

A horse can be driven on its own or as part of a pair, tandem or team. Competitions are held for all different types of driving horses and ponies.

The most exciting competition to watch is the marathon section of a driving trials – the horses are driven around a long course with obstacles. The driver needs to have complete control of the horses to avoid making any mistakes.

Make a lucky horseshoe

You will need:
• pen • cardboard • scissors
silver foil • string

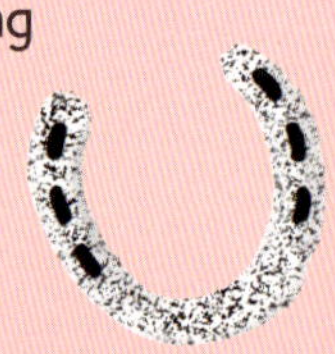

1. Draw a horseshoe shape onto the card. Ask an adult to help you cut out the shape.
2. Carefully cover the card shape with silver foil and smooth over. With the pen draw detail on to the horseshoe including nail holes.
3. Ask an adult to make two holes in the top of the horseshoe. Thread string through the holes to make a handle.

▲ Bay horses

▲ Polo pony

▲ Horseshoe

▲ Exmoor pony

▲ Driving pony

▲ Grooming Kit

▲ Shetland pony

▲ Zebra and foal

Horses and ponies

▼ Bay horses

◄ Polo pony

◄ Horseshoe

▼ Exmoor pony

▼ Driving pony

▲ Grooming Kit

▲ Shetland pony

▲ Zebra and foal

Horses and ponies

▲ Chestnut pony

▲ Saddle

▲ Lipizzaner

▲ Skewbald pony

▲ Pony friends

▲ Donkey foal

▲ Horse in winter rug

▲ Western riding

◄ Chestnut pony

▲ Skewbald pony

▲ Saddle

▲ Lipizzaner

► Pony friends

▲ Donkey foal

▼ Horse in winter rug

► Western riding

◀ Mounted games

▶ Apples

▼ Appaloosa mare and foal

▲ Cantering horse

▼ Heavy horses

▲ Shire horse

▼ Arab

▶ Tack

▲ Mounted games

▲ Apples

▲ Appaloosa mare and foal

▲ Cantering horse

▲ Heavy horses

▲ Shire horse

▲ Arab

▲ Tack

Horses and ponies

▶ Barrel racing

▼ Grey pony

▼ Haflinger mare and foal

▼ Racehorse

▼ Riding hat

▲ Hackney

▲ Eventing

▲ Morgan horse

▲ Barrel racing

▲ Grey pony

▲ Haflinger mare and foal

▲ Racehorse

▲ Riding hat

▲ Hackney

▲ Eventing

▲ Morgan horse

Jump off!

Showjumping is an exciting sport where horses and riders jump over a course of special obstacles or fences. The course is made up of a series of different types of obstacles including brightly coloured poles and planks, decorated fillers, solid walls and even water jumps!

To win a competition, the horse and rider must clear all the fences first time without knocking them down – this is called jumping a clear round. If a horse knocks a fence down or does not jump it at the first attempt, it is given a penalty score or fault.

If more than one horse jumps a clear round then they all ride over a shorter course and the fastest time wins. Winning horses and riders are given rosettes and sometimes a trophy or cup.

Horses and ponies

▶ Mounted games

This pony and rider are competing in a flag race, where the rider has to pick up a flag and move it to the next cone – the fastest combination wins the race

▶ Apples

Apples can be fed in small quantities to add interest to a horse's diet

◀ Cantering

This horse is enjoying the freedom of being turned out in its field

▲ Appaloosa mare and foal

This breed of horse has a beautiful spotted coat

▶ Shire horse

These large horses often have their manes decorated for shows

▲ Heavy horses

Working as a team these horses are powerful enough to pull heavy farming equipment

▶ Arab horse

Arab horses are often lively and high-spirited, they need experienced owners to care for them

▶ Tack

Wearing a saddle, bridle and exercise rug, this horse is ready to be ridden

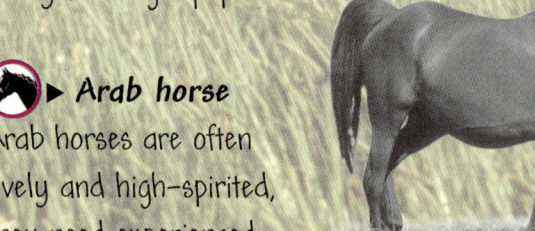

KEY: 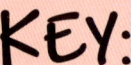 In the field    Horse care    At work    Relatives

 **► Barrel racing**
Barrel racing is a fast and exciting sport where horses race around three barrels in a clover-leaf shape

▲ Grey pony
The coat of a grey pony is made up of light and dark hairs, as the pony gets older more white hairs usually appear

▲ Riding hat
An approved safety hat should always be worn for horse riding

► Hackney
These high-stepping ponies are popular for driving

▲ Haflinger mare and foal
Haflingers are small and strong – they are palomino or chestnut with a light-coloured mane and tail

► Eventing
Competitors compete in dressage, cross-country and showjumping at these events

◄ Morgan horse
This breed is noted for its gentle temperament – it is a popular ridden show horse

▲ Racehorse
Racehorses are specially bred for speed and endurance

Many horses and ponies seem to be frightened of pigs!

Biggest and best

The Arab horse breed is unique in that it has 17 ribs – one less than other breeds.

The oldest horse on record is Old Billy, who died in November 1882 at the age of 62.

Horseracing is often called 'the sport of kings' because English kings of the 15th century encouraged the development of racing and the breeding of Thoroughbreds.

Read more about some record-breaking horses and ponies around the world

• The tallest horse on record is a huge Shire horse called Samson. He measured just over 21.2 hands (219 centimetres) in height!

• At the famous Spanish Riding School in Vienna, horses are trained to perform spectacular movements including leaping high in the air with a rider on them!

• The Shetland pony is the smallest of the British pony breeds. These small, hardy ponies have an average height of only 40 inches (102 centimetres).

Q: Where do you take a sick horse?
A: To the horse-pital!

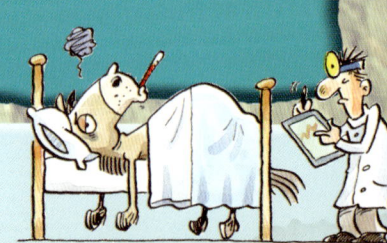

Horse care

Discover some important facts about caring for a horse or pony

- A pony's feet should be cleaned out twice a day to ensure there are no stones, sticks or mud trapped under the foot. A special tool called a hoof pick is used for this job.

- Most ponies enjoy being groomed and a short daily grooming session is beneficial for coat condition and muscle tone. Different brushes can be used: a dandy brush has stiff bristles and is used for removing mud from a winter coat, a body brush is softer and is used for removing dust from a summer or fine coat.

- Carrots make a tasty snack for a pony. They should be sliced in long, thin strips so the pony can easily chew them.

Welsh ponies have been bred in the Welsh mountains since before Roman times.

In 680BC, chariot racing was the first horse sport to be included at the Olympic Games.

The horseback sport of polocrosse developed from a combination of two other sports – polo and lacrosse.

Q: Why did the pony keeping coughing?
A: Because he was a little hoarse!

Fun facts

 Wild horses and ponies were present in the New Forest, England as early as 1016.

 In Roman times, white horses were thought to be a symbol of the gods and power.

 In 1947, the funeral of the famous US racehorse Man o'War was attended by over 2000 people.

Test your memory!

How much can you remember from your horses and ponies sticker activity book? Find out below!

1. What was the name of the oldest horse on record?
2. How many ribs does an Arab horse have: 16, 17 or 18?
3. In Roman times were white horses thought to be powerful or weak?
4. What sport is often called 'the sport of kings'?
5. How often should a pony's feet be cleaned out: twice daily, weekly or monthly?
6. Which was the first horse sport to be included in the Olympic Games?
7. Which is the smallest British pony breed: Exmoor, Shetland or Highland pony?
8. What does a red ribbon on a horse's tail mean?
9. Does a horse take one, two or three breaths with every canter stride ?
10. How many people attended the funeral of the racehorse Man o'War?

Q: What do you call a horse who lives next door?
A: A neigh-bour!

11. What breed of horse usually has a spotted coat: Appaloosa, Arab or Thoroughbred?

12. Does a polo pony need to be slow and sedate or fast and agile?

13. What breed of horse is used at the Spanish Riding School?

14. Should apples be fed to horses in small or large quantities?

15. Does a grey pony usually become lighter or darker as it grows older?

16. Which is bigger: a Shire or a Shetland?

17. Does a bay pony have a dark- or light-coloured mane and tail?

18. Does a Hackney pony have a high-stepping or long, flowing action?

19. What is the name of a traditional Western rider's hat?

20. What is a male donkey called?

Answers:

1. Old Billy 2. 11 3. Powerful 4. Horseracing 5. Twice daily 6. Chariot racing 7. Shetland pony 8. The horse might kick out 9. One 10. Over 2000 11. Appaloosa 12. Fast and agile 13. Lipizzaner 14. Small quantities 15. Lighter 16. Shire 17. Dark 18. High-stepping 19. Stetson 20. Jack

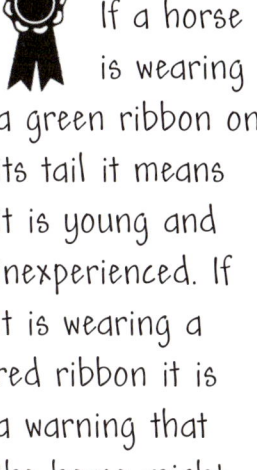

If a horse is wearing a green ribbon on its tail it means it is young and inexperienced. If it is wearing a red ribbon it is a warning that the horse might kick out.

When a horse is cantering, it takes a breath with every stride.

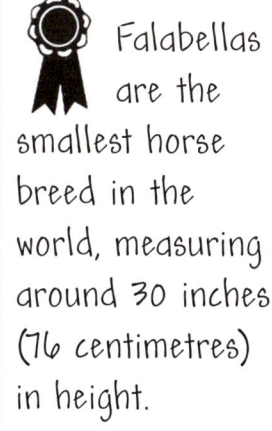

Falabellas are the smallest horse breed in the world, measuring around 30 inches (76 centimetres) in height.

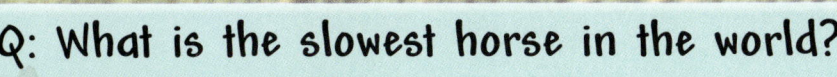

Q: What is the slowest horse in the world?
A: A clothes horse!

Other sticker books

You can now have more fun and collect all the sticker books in this series

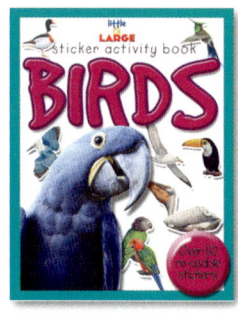

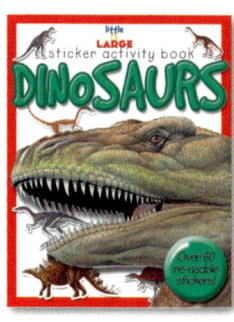

ISBN: 1-84236-304-2

ISBN: 1-84236-302-6

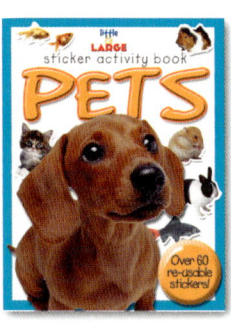

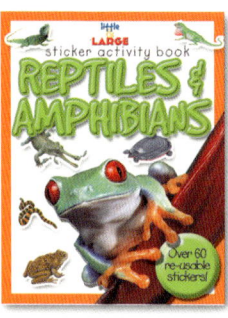

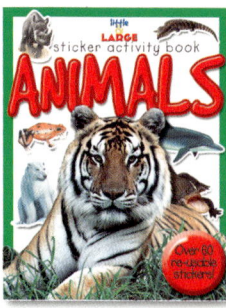

ISBN: 1-84236-305-0

ISBN: 1-84236-306-9

ISBN: 1-84236-254-2

ISBN: 1-84236-307-7

ISBN: 1-84236-303-4

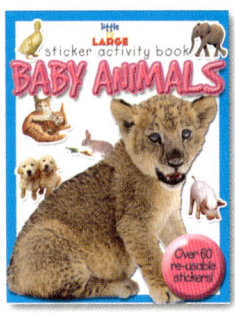

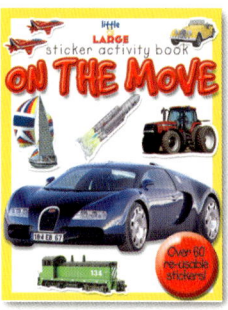

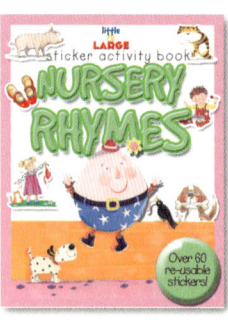

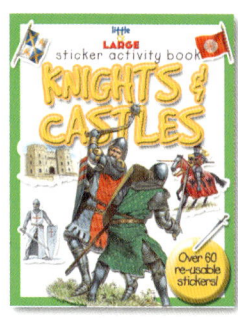

ISBN: 1-84236-244-5

ISBN: 1-84236-245-3

ISBN: 1-84236-247-X

ISBN: 1-84236-246-1

ISBN: 1-84236-255-0

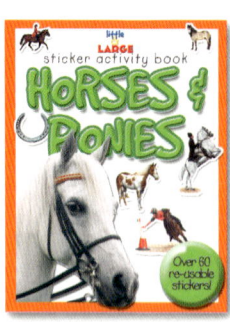

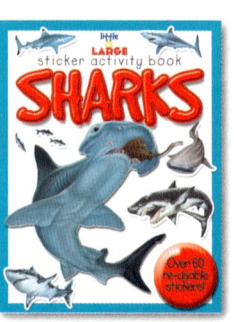

ISBN: 1-84236-498-7

ISBN: 1-84236-513-4

ISBN: 1-84236-514-2

ISBN: 1-84236-512-6

ISBN: 1-84236-515-0